D0568048

Christmas – 96
Rosemary – hope you
find lots of yommy things
to make! Love Judith

THE
VICTORIAN KITCHEN
Book of
JAMS AND JELLIES

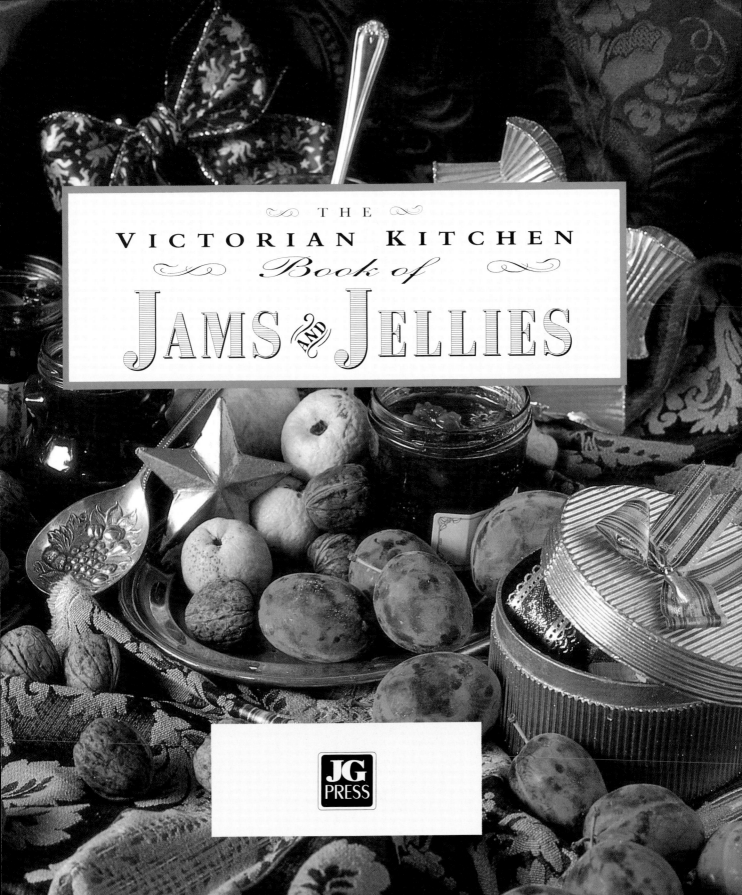

THE VICTORIAN KITCHEN
Book of
JAMS & JELLIES

JG
PRESS

The Victorian Kitchen Book Collection

Designed, written and edited by
THE BRIDGEWATER BOOK COMPANY LTD

Text *Amelia Swann*
Art Director *Annie Moss*
Designer *Jane Lanaway*
Managing Editor *Anna Clarkson*
Page make-up *Chris Lanaway*
Photographer *Trevor Wood*
Hand-colored plates *Lorraine Harrison*
Food preparation and styling *Jon Higgins*

Every effort has been made to trace all copyright
holders. The publishers sincerely apologise for
any inadvertant omissions and will be happy to
correct them in any future edition.

CLB 4185

Published in the USA 1995 by JG Press
Distributed by World Publications, Inc.

The JG Press imprint is a trademark of
JG Press, Inc
455 Somerset Avenue
North Dighton, MA 02764

Color separation by Sussex Repro, England
Printed and bound in Singapore

ISBN1-57215-048-3

CONTENTS

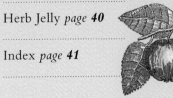

INTRODUCTION

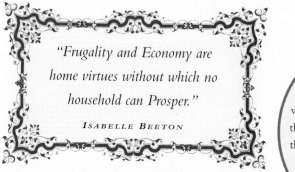

"Frugality and Economy are home virtues without which no household can Prosper."

ISABELLE BEETON

PRESERVING FRUIT IN JAM OR JELLY began in the 18th century, when glass technology and the availability of cheap, good quality sugar came together. Until the beginning of the 20th century, jam-making remained a home-based industry. The Victorians, in particular, made great use of seasonal fruits to make jams – for cakes and puddings as well as for the tea table – showing the sort of frugality and economy of which Mrs. Beeton would have approved.

From the grand houses, where huge armies of domestic staff bottled the fruits of the kitchen gardens, and the housekeeper made the best of market fruit that was in season, to the humblest cottage housewife using hedgerow fruits, jam-making was a seasonal ritual in every Victorian kitchen.

The recipes in this book try to capture the variety of jams, jellies, curds, and cheeses made by Victorian cooks, and show how they can be made in the modern kitchen. The recipes are based on authentic Victorian sources. Where possible, the yield you can expect is indicated; in the case of many of the jellies, however, the amount you can expect will vary according to the juiciness of the fruit you use.

Great care must be taken that syrups do not boil over, and that boiling is not carried to such an extent as to burn the sugar.

MRS BEETON

ELIZA ACTON'S JAM HINTS

Eliza Acton gave firmly practical directions for jam-making; here are a few of them rendered in modern English.

1 **Make sure that all pans, bottles and utensils are clean and dry.**
2 **Never put preserving pans on direct heat, but rest them on a trivet.**
3 **Stir jams constantly once the sugar is added until setting point is reached.**
4 **Clear scum as it rises.**
5 **Boil fruit rapidly to reduce it before adding sugar; this retains color and flavor. Do not make the purée so thick that sugar will not dissolve in it.**
6 **Never use tin, iron, or pewter utensils.**

Fruits intended for preservation should be gathered in the morning in dry weather ... with the morning sun on them if possible. They will then have their fullest flavour and keep in good condition longer than when gathered at any other time.

MRS. BEETON

The Setting Point

The setting point of jam is around 220°F. For precision testing use a sugar thermometer; immerse it in hot water first, and do not let it touch the bottom of the pan. A simpler way is the cold saucer test. Boil the jam for 20 minutes (unless otherwise indicated), then remove the pan from the heat. Drop a teaspoonful of the jam mixture on a saucer that has been cooling in the refrigerator. Leave to cool for a few minutes. If it forms a skin that wrinkles when you push it with a finger, the jam is set.

Preparing the Jars

Jars or bottles for jam should be well washed, rinsed, dried, and put into a slow oven to warm before they are filled. Never stand jars on a cold surface to fill them. Once the jars are filled, you must either cover them immediately, or wait until the jam is cold. Covering warm jam encourages mold. If using screwtop jars, put them on immediately. If using waxed discs and a second paper cover, put the discs on the jam when it is hot and then let it cool before adding the secondary covers. Label and date the jars immediately.

JAMS AND JELLIES

What's the Difference?

Jam is a mixture of fruit and sugar, boiled together
until most of the moisture is gone. Jelly is a mixture
of the juice from strained, boiled fruit, and sugar,
boiled together until the mixture jells. A preserve is
usually made with one kind of fruit only, bottled
whole or cut in half in a soft sugar syrup. Conserves
usually contain two or more fruits and are
stiff but spreadable, like a jam.

EVERYTHING YOU NEED TO MAKE JAMS
AND JELLIES IN THE VICTORIAN STYLE

STRAWBERRY JAM

Strawberry jam is a long-established favorite, as popular at the Victorian tea table as it is today. This is an adaptation of a recipe from Mrs. Beeton. Eliza Acton provides a similar version. The secret is to keep the fruit whole and luscious.

COOK'S TIP

As an alternative to lemon juice, Victorian cooks sometimes used 1 cup of fresh redcurrant juice per 1lb. of strawberries. If this method is used, allow the mixture to simmer for an extra 10 minutes.

INGREDIENTS

19 cups Well-ripened Strawberries
Juice of 2 Lemons
13³⁄₄ cups Sugar

MAKES APPROX. 8 CUPS

METHOD

❦ Hull the strawberries, removing any that are too ripe, and then rinse the remainder. Place them in a preserving pan with the lemon juice and cook over a low heat until some of the juice runs from the fruit. Take care not to break the strawberries up, as the beauty of a good strawberry jam is seeing and tasting the whole fruit.

❦ Add the sifted sugar and stir making sure it has dissolved completely, then simmer gently for 30 minutes. Remove any scum that rises to the top, and stir occasionally to prevent burning.

❦ When setting point is reached, put the jam into sterilized jars and seal tightly.

Growing strawberry plants in ornamental pots made an elegant centerpiece.

Indeed I feel as if I came too soon
To round your young May moon
And set the world a-gasping at my noon
Yet come I must, so here are strawberries,
Sun flushed and sweet, as many as you please
And here are full blown roses by the score
More roses, and yet more.

CHRISTINA ROSSETTI

STRAWBERRY JAM,
EVERYBODY'S FAVORITE

The Delights of Strawberry Picking

Here is Mrs Elton, upwardly mobile wife of the vicar of Highbury in all her apparatus of happiness on a strawberry picking outing at Donwell Abbey. "Strawberries and only strawberries could now be thought of, or spoken of. 'The best fruit in England – everybody's favourite – always wholesome – These the finest beds and finest sorts. Delightful to gather for oneself – the only way of really enjoying them. Morning decidely the best time – never tired – every sort good – hautboy infinitely superior – no comparison the others hardly eatable – hautboys very scarce – Chili preferred – white wood finest flavour of all – price of strawberries in London – abundance about Bristol – Maple Grove – cultivation – beds when to be renewed – gardeners thinking exactly different – no general rule – gardeners never to be put out of their way – delicious fruit – only too rich to be eaten much of – inferior to cherries – currants more refreshing –only objection to gathering strawberries the stooping – glaring sun – tired to death – could bear it no longer – must go and sit in the shade.' "

EMMA, JANE AUSTEN

Hautboys refers to the hautbois strawberry, a relative of the small, delicious Alpine strawberry and the rootstock for the European strawberry. Chilis were larger fruits native to South America, which were imported to France and thence the rest of Europe by an army officer named Fréziers.

A SUMPTUOUS COLLECTION OF FRUIT JELLIES

BLACKCURRANT JAM

Eliza Acton observed that "no fruit jellies so easily as black currants when they are ripe." She advocated a minimum of water in her recipe; Mrs. Beeton was more cautious. This is an adaptation of her recipe.

COOK'S TIP

Mrs. Beeton warns that "great attention must be paid to the stirring of this jam as it is very liable to burn on account of the thickness of the juice."

INGREDIENTS

12 cups Fresh Blackcurrants
6 cups Fresh Cold Water
14 cups Sugar

MAKES ABOUT 11 CUPS

METHOD

❦ Thoroughly wash the blackcurrants, removing all stalks and leaves. Place the fruit in a preserving pan and cover with the fresh water.

❦ Bring to the boil, then reduce to a simmer to allow the fruit to soften. This should take approximately 30 minutes.

❦ Once the fruit is soft, remove the pan from the heat, add the sugar, and stir thoroughly until dissolved. Return the pan to the heat and cook rapidly until setting point is reached; pot and seal.

WHITECURRANT JAM

"A beautiful preserve."
This is how Eliza Acton described this jam. A version of her recipe is given below. Whitecurrants are less readily available today, but it is worth seeking them out to make this unusual, delicate preserve.

INGREDIENTS

12 cups Fresh Whitecurrants
9 cups Sugar
Juice of 1 Lemon

MAKES ABOUT 8 CUPS

METHOD

❦ Thoroughly wash the whitecurrants under fresh running water removing any stalk or leaf still remaining. Place the cleaned fruit in a preserving pan along with the sugar.

❦ Bring to the boil and cook for 5 to 10 minutes stirring continuously but carefully, just before setting point is reached stir in the lemon juice.

❦ Pot into warm, sterilized jars, and seal tightly.

REDCURRANT JELLY

Preparing redcurrants is a time consuming task, but the jelly produced is well worth it. This is a version of Eliza Acton's "Norman receipt". She points out that in Normandy, "where the fruit is of richer quality, this preserve is boiled for only two minutes and is both firm and beautifully transparent."

INGREDIENTS
10 cups Fresh Redcurrants
7 cups Caster Sugar

METHOD

❦ Thoroughly wash the fruit and carefully remove all the currants from the stalks. Place in a preserving pan with the sugar and mix thoroughly.

❦ Bring to the boil and cook rapidly for 8 minutes, stirring all the time and removing any scum lying on the surface.

❦ Pour the contents of the pan through a clean sieve to remove the remains of the currants, and pot the jelly into small jars.

COOK'S TIP

Do not worry if your jelly is rather soft when you come to use it, as Eliza Acton commented "the jelly is scarcely firm enough for the table," but is "valuable for many purposes, and always agreeable eating."

Nursery Preserve

A useful "nursery preserve" may be made from the redcurrants left in the sieve. If they are not squeezed too dry, Mrs. Beeton suggests you add a few fresh raspberries to the redcurrant pulp and boil them together with enough sugar to sweeten. The preserve should not be stored, but eaten on the same day as a pudding sauce or a jam for children.

Blackcurrants

There are few preparations of fruit so refreshing and so useful in illness as those of blackcurrants, and it is therefore advisable always to have a store of them and to have them well and carefully made.

ELIZA ACTON

RASPBERRY JAM

Eliza Acton considered raspberry jam to be "a very favourite English preserve" and, cheeringly, "one of the most easily made that can be." This is an adaptation of her recipe for "an excellent jam for common family use."

COOK'S TIP

As for Strawberry Jam, it is very important not to overcook Raspberry Jam, as part of its beauty is in its deep red colouring.

INGREDIENTS

16 cups Very Fresh Raspberries

9 cups Preserving Sugar

MAKES ABOUT 8 CUPS

METHOD

❦ Wash the raspberries thoroughly and remove any stalks or leaves. Carefully pick over the fruit to remove any moldy raspberries.

❦ Put the fruit into a preserving pan and heat gently until the raspberries start to break up, then remove from the heat and stir in the sugar until completely dissolved. Return to the heat and boil rapidly for 5 minutes, until setting point has been reached.

❦ Pot into warm sterilized jars, and seal tightly.

RASPBERRY CURD

Fruit curds come from a tradition older than the Victorians. They were a country treat, made in small quanities as they would not keep for long. Mrs Beeton gives a few sample recipes, but curds have now come back into their own because they can be stored in the refrigerator for up to three months.

INGREDIENTS

6 cups Fresh Raspberries

2 Cooking Apples

1 cup Unsalted Butter

Fresh Cold Water

4 eggs

2¼ cups Caster Sugar

MAKES ABOUT 3 CUPS

METHOD

❦ Wash the raspberries and apples and roughly chop the latter into small pieces. Place in a preserving pan with a small amount of water and cook until the fruit becomes a pulp.

❦ Remove from the heat and pass this purée through a sieve to remove all skin and seeds, and place in a bowl over hot water. Add the chopped butter and sugar, and stir until they have dissolved into the fruit. Lightly beat the eggs and add to the pan.

❦ Cook until the curd thickens, but do not allow the mixture to boil.

❦ Pot into small jars and cover.

The Barberry, raspberry and gooseberry too,
Look now to be planted, as other things do
The gooseberry, raspberry and roses all three.
With strawberries under them, trimly agree.

THOMAS TUSSER

RASPBERRY JAM, REFRESHINGLY EXCELLENT ON BREAD OR IN TARTLETS.

BOTH THE SCENT AND FLAVOUR OF THIS
FRUIT ARE VERY REFRESHING, AND THE
BERRY ITSELF IS EXCEEDINGLY WHOLESOME
AND INVALUABLE TO PEOPLE OF A
NERVOUS OR BILIOUS TEMPERAMENT.
ITS JUICE IS RICH AND ABUNDANT, AND
TO MANY EXTREMELY AGREEABLE.

Mrs. Beeton on raspberries.

SMOOTH AND CREAMY RASPBERRY CURD

THE INDUSTRIAL GOOSEBERRY

*The plebian origin of the Gooseberry has been,
I fear, a handicap to its appreciation at
cultured tables.*

This observation was made by Edward Ashdown Bunyard in his
Anatomy of Dessert. As he pointed out, "The big gooseberry was
born in the smoke and moisture of Macclesfield and other great
industrial towns." The gooseberry, although growing well
thoughout northern Europe and up as far as the Arctic circle, is
nowhere more appreciated than in England. In the early 19th
century, workers in the Midlands took to growing gooseberries,
raising them from seedlings, to enter into fiercely fought
competitions. Their endeavors produced large, flavorsome
gooseberries of the kind that are now grown commercially.

GREEN GOOSEBERRY JAM

This adaptation of an Eliza Acton recipe makes a jam that is, in her words, "firm and of good colour". She points out that a seedless version would be "very excellent", but that this is quite delicious enough.

INGREDIENTS

16 cups Fresh Gooseberries
3 cups Fresh Cold Water
11⅓ cups Sugar

MAKES ABOUT 8 CUPS

METHOD

❧ Remove the stalks from the gooseberries and wash thoroughly. Place the fruit in a preserving pan and cover with the fresh water, bring to the boil and then reduce to a simmer until the fruit has taken on a soft consistency. This takes about 30 minutes.

❧ Remove the pan from the heat and stir in the sugar until it has completely dissolved. Return the pan to the heat and boil rapidly for 30 minutes or until setting point is reached, stirring regularly and removing any surface scum as necessary.

COOK'S TIP

Eliza Acton observed, "this makes a fine and refreshing preserve if the fruit be rubbed through a sieve before the sugar is added. If well reduced afterwards it may be used in a gateaux," by which she means fruit paste.

GREEN GOOSEBERRY JELLY

This is another recipe from Eliza Acton, who seems to have been extremely partial to goosberries. They are a peculiarly English fruit – although they are also grown in parts of France – and there are many Victorian recipes that use them. This makes a sweetly tart jelly: try it as an accompaniment to smoked or kippered mackerel.

INGREDIENTS

16 cups Fresh Gooseberries
6 cups Fresh Cold Water
Sugar

METHOD

❧ Wash the gooseberries and remove the tops and stalks. Place in a preserving pan with the water and simmer on a medium heat until the fruit is well cooked and very soft. Pour the contents of the pan into a jelly bag and let the juices strain slowly for several hours. Do not press the fruit through.

❧ Measure the juice and return it to the pan, boil for 15 minutes longer to allow the liquid to reduce. Remove the pan from the heat and add 3 cups of sugar to every 2 cups of juice measured earlier. Stir well to make sure it dissolves completely. Continue boiling until setting point is reached, removing surface scum as necessary, and pour into small, sterilized jars.

MARROW SQUASH JAM

Vegetable marrows came to England in the mid-19th century, where they were seized upon by kitchen gardeners as a versatile, economic vegetable. Relatively tasteless themselves, they can be used to bulk out stews, to pickle or to make excellent jam. Use old, woody marrows for jam-making, as the sugar softens them well.

INGREDIENTS

1 x 4lb. Marrow Squash
9 cups Sugar
Fresh Root Ginger

MAKES ABOUT 8 CUPS

METHOD

❧ Peel the squash, cut into small cubes, and spread out on a large baking sheet. Cover with the sugar and put to one side for 24 hours; this allows time for the sugar to draw the moisture from the squash.

❧ Place all the squash, sugar, and liquid into a preserving pan and bring to the boil. Add the peeled and bruised root ginger and continue to boil until setting point is reached. Remove the ginger and pot into warm, sterilized jars. Cover and seal.

COOK'S TIP

Add the rind and juice of one lemon to every 2lb. of squash for an extra tang.

GREENGAGE JAM

The greengage, being a kind of plum, belongs to the family of the Victorians' favorite fruit. Mrs. Beeton gives a recipe for greengages in syrup, but this jam will keep for longer. Try to find old-fashioned varieties of greengages if you can; they have an excellent flavor.

INGREDIENTS

16 cups Fresh Greengages

9 cups Sugar

1½ cups Fresh Water

MAKES ABOUT 8 CUPS

METHOD

❦ Wash the greengages thoroughly, cut each one in half and remove the stone. Put the stones to one side. Place the fruit in a preserving pan and pour over the water. Bring to the boil then reduce to a simmer until the fruit has cooked to a pulp.

❦ Break open half a dozen stones and remove the kernels. These should be immersed in boiling water for 5 minutes, then split in half and added to the fruit mixture.

❦ Remove the pan from the heat and add the sugar. This mixture should then be boiled until setting point is reached, taking care to remove any surface scum that may appear.

❦ Pot and seal.

The greengage is a variety of plum named in honor of the Gage family, a 17th-century dynasty of soldier-diplomats and travelers, who bought the fruit to England from France, where it is still known as the *Reine-Claude*.

As Mrs. Beeton points out, it can be "agreeable at dessert, when perfectly ripe," and she approved of the baking and preserving of the fruit to banish any "bad qualities". In her *Book of Household Management* she gives a recipe for greengages in syrup in which the halved fruits bathe in a light sugar syrup. It does not last as long as the jam, but it is just as delicious.

GREENGAGE JAM, CLOTTED CREAM AND SCONES FOR TEA

Rose Petal Jam

This is a gorgeous, delicate treat, fragrant and very sweet, the perfect preserve for a Victorian maiden. Only a tiny amount is needed. It tastes divine with thick clotted cream on warm scones or as a filling for sponge cakes. Petals from damask roses give the most aromatic jam.

INGREDIENTS

4 cups Petals taken from your Favorite Rosebush

2¼ cups Sugar

Juice of 1 Lemon

1 cup Fresh Water

MAKES ABOUT 1⅓ CUPS

METHOD

❦ Cut away the bottom of each petal, as this part can make the jam taste bitter. Place the petals in a preserving pan and pour over the water. Heat very gently for about 30 minutes to extract the color and fragrance and then remove the petals and put aside.

❦ Add the sugar and lemon juice to the pan and make sure all the sugar has dissolved. Boil the mixture rapidly, allowing most of the liquid to evaporate.

❦ When you are left with a very thick syrup, put the petals back in and stir through the mixture to distribute evenly. As only a small amount of this jam is used at any one time, it is better kept in small, 4oz jars.

The rose was awake
all night for your sake
Knowing your promise to me
The lilies and roses were all awake
They signed for the dawn
and thee.

MAUD, ALFRED LORD TENNYSON

ALAS THAT SPRING SHOULD VANISH
WITH THE ROSE
THAT YOUTH'S SWEET-SCENTED MANUSCRIPT
SHOULD CLOSE!
THE NIGHTINGALE THAT IN THE BRANCHES SANG,
AH, WHENCE, AND WHITHER FLOWN AGAIN, WHO KNOWS!

EACH MORN A THOUSAND ROSES BRING, YOU SAY
YES, BUT WHERE LEAVES OF THE ROSE OF YESTERDAY?

From *The Rubaiyat of Omar Khayyam of Naishapur*
Translated by Edward Fitzgerald (1809–1883)

These verses, translated from the romantic melancholy
quatrain of Omar Khayyam, an 11th-century astronomer
and poet, took the Victorian reading classes by storm.
Fitzgerald's rendering of the plangent themes of
transient beauty and the fleeting but fragrant
pleasures of love struck a great chord in the
Victorian heart, and inspired a love of all things
Eastern and respectably exotic.

GOLDEN APRICOT JAM, DELICIOUS ON HOT BUTTERED TOAST

APRICOT JAM

Apricots were another favorite Victorian fruit, and grew well in hothouses and conservatories. This is an adaptation of Mrs. Beeton's recipe. She recommended that the halved apricots should be spread over trays, sprinkled with sugar, and left to marinate for 12 hours before the whole lot was tipped into the preserving pan. This version is less time-consuming and just as delicious.

INGREDIENTS

4lb. Fresh Ripe Apricots
2 cups Fresh Water
9 cups Sugar

MAKES ABOUT 8 CUPS

METHOD

❧ Wash the apricots and cut them in half to remove the stone; put the stones to one side. Place the apricots, water, and sugar into a preserving pan and cook on a moderate heat so the fruit does not break up too much.

❧ Meanwhile, crack open the stones and remove the kernels. These should be added to the pan as they impart a very special flavor. When the apricots appear cooked, remove them from the pan and distribute evenly among the prepared jars.

❧ When all the apricots are removed, boil the syrup rapidly until setting point has been reached, taking care to remove any scum that may have risen to the top. Pour the syrup and kernels over the fruit, then seal tightly.

Cherry Jam

This is an adaptation of Eliza Acton's recipe. She made it with Kentish or Flemish cherries, but Morello cherries or amarelles can be used by modern cooks. Take care not to boil it too long or use too much sugar, as this can spoil both the color and the flavor.

INGREDIENTS

13 ¾ cups Black Cherries
8 cups Sugar
Juice of 2 Lemons

MAKES ABOUT 10 ½ CUPS

METHOD

❦ Wash and stone the cherries. Place in a preserving pan with the lemon juice, and gently stew on a low heat for 15 minutes to allow the juices to run from the fruit.
❦ Turn up the heat and boil the cherries rapidly for approximately 45 minutes, stirring continuously, until much of the juice has evaporated. Add the sugar away from the heat and make sure it has dissolved completely.
❦ Return the pan to the heat and once again boil rapidly for 20 minutes until setting point is reached, stirring and removing any surface scum as necessary. Pot into warm, sterilized jars and seal.

COOK'S TIP

It is worth noting a comment of Eliza Acton's: "Cherries which are bruised will not make good preserves, they will always remain tough."

IF SO BE YOU ASK ME WHERE
THEY DO GROW? I ANSWER THERE
WHERE MY JULIA'S LIPS DO SMILE,
THERE'S THE LAND OF CHERRY ISLE.

Robert Herrick

SO WE GREW TOGETHER
LIKE TO A DOUBLE CHERRY, SEEMING PARTED
BUT YET AS UNION IN PARTITION
TWO LOVELY BERRIES MOULDED ON ONE STEM.

A Midsummer Night's Dream,
William Shakespeare

Common Cherry Cheese

This is another cherry recipe from Eliza Acton. By "common" she means for everyday use, rather than "dull and ordinary." The cheese is very stiff and can be turned out from its mold in one piece. It is delicious served sliced, with whipped cream.

INGREDIENTS

9 cups Fresh Cherries
Sugar
Fresh Water

METHOD

❦ Pick over the cherries and remove any stalks or bruised fruit, then wash thoroughly. Place the fruit in a preserving pan and add a small amount of water to prevent burning. Place on the heat and cook until the fruit is soft and tender; this takes approximately 30 minutes.
❦ Pass the fruit purée through a sieve to remove the skin and stones and measure the cherry pulp before returning it to the pan to boil down to a dry paste. Remove the pan from the heat and add 1 cup of sugar to every 2 cups of cherry purée measured earlier. Stir until the sugar has completely dissolved, and then continue to cook until the cheese has a very dry texture. Pack into straight-sided pots or molds, and cover tightly.

ELIZA ACTON ALWAYS
STIPULATED FLEMISH OR KENTISH
CHERRIES IN HER RECIPES.

Kent, sir – everybody knows Kent – apples, cherries, hops and women.

MR JINGLE IN *Pickwick Papers,* CHARLES DICKENS

Loveliest of trees, the cherry now
Is hung with bloom along the bough.

A Shropshire Lad, A. E. HOUSMAN

PLUM JAM

The plums hung rich and heavy on the bough in Victorian orchards. Versatile, juicy, and abundant, plums of all kinds were the first choice when the Victorian cook was making jams, preserves, puddings, and cakes. This is an adaptation of Mrs. Beeton's recipe.

COOK'S TIP

To get that special taste in your plum jam, Mrs. Beeton recommends cracking open the stones and adding a few kernels to the jam just before it has finished cooking. This "imparts a very delicious flavour."

INGREDIENTS

4lb. Fresh Plums
2 cups Fresh Water
9 cups Sugar

MAKES ABOUT 8 CUPS

METHOD

❧ Wash the plums thoroughly and allow to drain. Cut the fruit in half, remove the stone and put the stones to one side. Place the fruit in a preserving pan and pour in the fresh water. Cook the fruit over a gentle heat until it has taken on a pulpy consistency.

❧ Remove and stir in the sugar, making sure it has completely dissolved before returning the pan to the heat and boiling rapidly until setting point is reached.

❧ Transfer to warm, sterilized jars, and seal tightly.

PLUMS, IN ALL THEIR VARIETIES, WERE THE
FAVORITE FRUIT OF THE VICTORIANS

RICH, DARK, DAMSON JAM, THICKLY SPREAD ON HOMEMADE BREAD, MADE A ROBUST TEA-TIME TREAT

THE DAMASCENE PLUM

The damson is a kind of plum.
It originally came from Damascus
and was called the "Damascene Plum."
According to Mrs. Beeton, "it combines
sugary and acid qualities in happy
proportions when fully ripe... Amongst the
list of the best sorts of baking plums, the
damson stands first, not only on account
of the abundance of its juice, but also on
account of its soon softening. Because
of the roughness of its flavour,
it requires a large quantity
of sugar."

DAMSON JAM

Damsons are robust, rustic members of the plum family and often grow wild. If you can find the old-fashioned, oval-shaped damsons with black skin and green flesh, use them for this jam, which is an adaptation from Eliza Acton's recipe.

INGREDIENTS

4lb. Ripe, Stoned Damsons

9 cups Sugar

MAKES ABOUT 10½ CUPS

METHOD

❦ Place the damsons in a preserving pan on a low heat and bring to the boil. Cook for 30 minutes until the fruit has broken down into a pulpy consistency. (At this point the fruit can be passed through a sieve if a smoother textured jam is required).

❦ Remove the pan from the heat and stir in the sugar, making sure it dissolves completely. Return the pan to the heat and boil for a further 15 minutes until the jam reaches its setting point.

❦ Pot into warm, sterilized jars, and seal tightly.

PRESERVED MULBERRIES

Mulberries were an old-fashioned fruit even to the Victorians. Today they are rare and short-seasoned, and although you can make a superb jam with them, packing them in syrup gives a more versatile preserve. They can be used in pies or tarts, or served warm with cream or homemade rice pudding.

INGREDIENTS

8 cups Fresh Mulberries

5³⁄₄ cups Sugar

Fresh Water

Mulberry juice stains very badly, so take care with your white linen.

METHOD

❦ Thoroughly wash and weigh out 1½ cups of the mulberries. Place them in a preserving pan with just enough water to cover, and cook until much of the juice is extracted, strain off the liquid and discard the fruit.

❦ Measure out 2½ cups of the liquor and pour back into a clean preserving pan, add the sugar, and bring to the boil, removing any surface scum when necessary. Remove the pan from the heat and stir in the remaining mulberries; these should be gently simmered for 15 minutes and then allowed to stand in the cooling syrup for 24 hours.

❦ The next day, reboil the fruit and syrup, and when setting point is reached, pot the preserved fruit into sterilized jars, and seal tightly.

Mulberries

GLASS THEY'LL BLOW YOU CRYSTAL CLEAR
WHERE JUST A TAINT CLOUD OF ROSE SHALL APPEAR
AS IF IN PURE WATER YOU DROPPED AND LET LIE
A BRUISED BLACK-BLOODED MULBERRY.

Robert Browning

GENUINE SCOTCH MARMALADE

This robust and manly marmalade is based on a recipe quoted by Eliza Acton. Although she did not make it herself, it was "guaranteed as an excellent one by the Scottish lady from whom it was procured." It makes a dark, pleasingly bitter preserve.

INGREDIENTS

3lb. Seville Oranges
14 cups Sugar
7½ cups Fresh Water
Juice of 2 Lemons
2 T. Black Treacle (optional)

MAKES ABOUT 13 CUPS

METHOD

❧ With a sharp knife cut all the oranges into quarters, remove the fruit from the skin, and cut into small chunks, removing all the seeds. Place to one side. If the oranges have thick skins, cut away some of the white inside the rind and slice the remainder into thin strips or chunks.

❧ Place the orange chunks and the strips of peel into a preserving pan along with the seeds, tied in muslin, and pour in the water. Bring to the boil and cook until the strips of peel are tender. Remove the seeds from the pan and add the lemon juice and sugar, stirring until it has dissolved.

❧ If desired, you can now add the black treacle. This gives a darker coloring to the marmalade and makes the flavor slightly bitter. Boil until the setting point has been reached. Pot in warm, sterilized jars, and seal.

ORANGE MARMALADE

Victorian kitchens were aromatic with the scent and zest of bitter Seville oranges during the short, frenetic marmalade-making season. The oranges were at their best in January and February, and so all marmalades had to be made quickly. Nowadays, you can freeze the oranges when they are in season and use them whenever you want. This is Mrs. Beeton's admirable marmalade.

INGREDIENTS

3lb. Seville Oranges
7 cups Sugar
3¾ cups Fresh Water

MAKES ABOUT 8 CUPS

METHOD

❧ Peel the skin from all the oranges with a sharp knife, trying not to remove too much pith. Boil the skins in a saucepan of water until tender; this should take about 2 hours.

❧ Cut the skin into matchstick strips and put to one side. Chop the flesh of the oranges into small pieces, discarding any seeds and white pith but saving the juice; put to one side also.

❧ In a preserving pan boil together the sugar and fresh water until all the sugar has melted and you are left with a clear liquid. Add the reserved skin, flesh and juice and boil for approximately 30 minutes until setting point is reached.

❧ Pot into warm, sterilized jars, and seal.

Marmalade comes from the Portuguese word *marmelada*, which means "quince conserve," from *marmelo*, the Portuguese word for quince. It soon came to mean any sweet jelly with fruit suspended in it.

Orange marmalade was said to have been invented for Katharine of Aragón, queen to Henry VIII of England, who missed the bright oranges of Spain. In French, a marmalade signifies any thick purée of fruit.

ORANGE AND LEMON MARMALADE BROUGHT A HINT OF SUMMER
SUN TO THE VICTORIAN PARLOR DURING THE WINTER MONTHS

CRAB APPLE JELLY

Crab Apple Jelly has been made forever. Every housewife had a recipe. Many cottage gardens were blessed with a crab apple tree or the fruit could be picked up for free, so this is an excellently frugal kind of preserve. It tastes very good with pork or cold meats.

INGREDIENTS
4lb. Crab Apples
5 cups Fresh Cold Water
Sugar

METHOD

❧ Thoroughly wash and chop the apples (there is no need to peel or core them) and place in a preserving pan. Cover with the water and bring to the boil. Cook until the fruit is very soft.

❧ Remove from the heat and strain the purée through a jelly bag for several hours, but do not squeeze the bag, as this will cloud your juice. Measure the juice and return to the pan with $2^{1}/_{4}$ cups of sugar to every 2 cups of apple.

❧ Stir over a gentle heat until the sugar has dissolved, then boil rapidly until setting point is reached. Pour the jelly into warm, sterilized jars, and seal tightly.

Medlars

MEDLARS ARE A NATIVE ENGLISH FRUIT WHICH GROW WILD IN THE HEDGES ABOUT MINISHALL IN CHESHIRE. THEY ARE KEPT IN MOIST BRAN FOR A FORTNIGHT BEFORE BEING ROTTEN ENOUGH TO EAT.

Child's Guide, 1850

MEDLAR CHEESE

Medlars are an ancient variety of pear. They once grew wild in England, but are now difficult to get ahold of, although some Greek grocers may have them. They have to be eaten when they are rotten, and have a sweet and sour wine-like taste. If you have never tried one, this cheese may make a good introduction.

INGREDIENTS

4lb. Fresh Medlars
Sugar
Fresh Water

METHOD

❦ Wash the medlars thoroughly and cut in half. Place the fruit in a preserving pan with a small amount of water to prevent burning. Cook on a moderate heat until the fruit has become soft and pulpy.

❦ Pass the fruit through a sieve to remove any skin and stone, and measure the pulp before returning it to the preserving pan to boil down to a dry paste. Remove the pan from the heat and add $2^{1/4}$ cup of sugar for every 2 cups of purée measured earlier, stirring to ensure the sugar has dissolved completely.

❦ Boil until the cheese has taken on a dry texture then pot into straight-sided jars or molds, and cover tightly.

LEMON AND ORANGE CURD

Like Raspberry Curd (see page 16), these are old-fashioned preserves. They were made to be eaten within the week. Today they should not be kept longer than three months, and should be very clearly labelled with their date of making. Their glowing opaque color make a lively addition to the tea table.

(see page 16)

COOK'S TIP

If you are making orange curd, it is a good idea to substitute a small amount of orange juice with lemon as this gives the curd a little bit of a "kick."

INGREDIENTS

6 Juicy Lemons or 4 Ripe Oranges
6 Fresh Eggs
1 cup Unsalted Butter
2 1/4 cups Caster Sugar

MAKES ABOUT 2 CUPS

METHOD

❦ Finely grate the peel of the fruit, then chop them in half and squeeze out all the juice, straining to remove all the seeds.

❦ Place in a pan over boiling water, add the chopped butter and caster sugar and stir to ensure they dissolve fully.

❦ Over a gentle heat add the strained, lightly beaten eggs and cook gently until the curd coats the back of a spoon. Pour into small, sterilized jars, and seal tightly.

Oranges and Lemons

ORANGE AND LEMONS	WHEN I GROW RICH
SAY THE BELLS OF ST CLEMENTS	SAY THE BELLS AT SHOREDITCH
YOU OWE ME FIVE FARTHINGS	WHEN WILL THAT BE?
SAY THE BELLS OF ST MARTINS	SAY THE BELLS OF STEPNEY
WHEN WILL YOU PAY ME?	I DO NOT KNOW
SAY THE BELLS AT OLD BAILEY	SAYS THE GREAT BELL AT BOW.

THICK AND TANGY ORANGE AND LEMON CURDS, THE ESSENCE OF LONG, HOT SUMMER DAYS

ORANGE AND HONEY MARMALADE

This recipe is adapted from Mrs. Beeton. Using honey instead of sugar means that no extra liquid is needed in the cooking.

INGREDIENTS

3lb. Seville Oranges
1⅓ cups Fresh Honey per 2½ cups Orange Pulp

MAKES ABOUT 5⅓ CUPS

METHOD

❧ Peel the skin from all the oranges with a sharp knife, place in a saucepan of water and boil until tender; this should take about 2 hours.

❧ Cut the skin into matchstick strips and put to one side. Chop the flesh of the oranges into small pieces, discarding any pips and white pith but saving the juice. Measure the pulp in a jug.

❧ In a preserving pan boil together the fruit pulp, rind, and honey for approximately 30 minutes, until setting point is reached.

❧ Pot into warm, sterilized jars, and seal.

ORANGE AND HONEY MARMALADE

Sloes are the fruit of the blackthorn. They are small, blue-black, and extremely sour. In country lore they have a medicinal role: they are said to cure cattle diseases and gumboils in humans. When preserved in gin – picked when the first frost has bruised their tough skins, and bottled in the alcohol – they were at their best. Sloe gin mixed with penny royal and valerian made "Mother's Ruin," the rural remedy for matrimonial excess.

SLOE AND APPLE JELLY

According to Mrs. Beeton, sloes "when ripe, make a good preserve." This is a fine-flavored jelly with a beautiful color. It is good with hare, rabbit, or other game.

INGREDIENTS

12 cups Sloes
2lb. Crab Apples
Fresh Cold Water
Sugar

METHOD

❧ Thoroughly wash the sloes and apples and cut the latter into chunks. Place the fruit in a preserving pan and pour over enough water to cover.

❧ Simmer over a low heat until the fruit has become soft and the juice is well extracted. Pour the contents of the pan into a jelly bag and allow to strain for several hours.

❧ Measure out the strained juice, and for every 2½ cups add 2½ cups of sugar. Boil these together in a preserving pan for approximately 30 minutes, removing any scum that may surface. When setting point is reached, pour into warm jars and seal tightly.

*They dined on mince
And slices of quince
Which they ate with a
runcible spoon;
And hand in hand on the
edge of the sand
They danced by the light
of the moon.*

EDWARD LEAR

QUINCE JELLY

This is based on an Eliza Acton recipe. The jelly should be firm emough to turn out of its pot or mold in its entirety, and will be "beautifully transparent, and rich in flavour."
This wonderfully rich jelly is an excellent alternative to redcurrant jelly to eat with meat.

INGREDIENTS

*4lb. Fresh Quinces
Fresh Water
Sugar*

METHOD

❧ Thoroughly clean and roughly chop the quinces. Place the fruit in a preserving pan and cover with water. Slowly bring to the boil and cook until the quinces are soft; this takes about an hour.

❧ Pour the contents of the pan into a jelly bag and allow the juices to strain for several hours. Measure the juices that collect and return them to the cleaned pan, bring back to the boil, and add $2^{1}/_{4}$ cups of sugar for each $2^{1}/_{2}$ cups of liquid, stirring to ensure it has dissolved fully.

❧ Continue boiling until setting point is reached, removing any scum as necessary. Pour into pots and tightly seal.

QUINCE MARMALADE

Quinces are an ancient fruit, distantly related to apples and pears. They smell sweet but taste tart, and are not to be eaten raw. Their high pectin content makes them an excellent choice for all sorts of jams, marmalades, preserves, and jellies. This is an adaptation of Eliza Acton's recipe.

INGREDIENTS

*4lb. Fresh Quinces
9 cups Sugar
Fresh Water*

MAKES ABOUT 10½ CUPS

METHOD

❧ Take approximately one pound in weight of the quinces and cut into quarters. Remove the core and seeds and place in a heavy-bottomed saucepan. Add to the pan just enough cold water to cover the fruit, and boil until the quinces just begin to break up. Strain off the cooking liquor and reserve $3^{3}/_{4}$ cups.

❧ Meanwhile, prepare the rest of the quinces as before and cook gently in the reserved liquor until they are soft and pulpy. Press all the fruit and liquor through a sieve and return to the heat in a preserving pan. Cook until most of the moisture has evaporated, then add the sugar and boil rapidly for 30 minutes, stirring continuously.

❧ Pot into sterilized jars and seal.

APPLE JELLY

◦≈◦

This is Mrs. Beeton's recipe for a thoroughly sensible, all-around
domestic jelly. As she says, "this preparation is useful for
garnishing sweet dishes and may be turned out for dessert."
It can also be eaten with savory dishes.

INGREDIENTS
4lb. Apples
7½ cups Fresh Cold Water
Sugar

◦≈◦

METHOD

❦ Thoroughly wash the apples. Remove the peel and core and then
thinly slice. Place in a preserving pan and pour over the water.
Simmer over a low heat until the fruit has become soft and the juice
is well extracted.

❦ Pour the contents of the pan into a jelly bag and allow to strain for
several hours. Measure out the strained juice and for every 2½ cups
add 2¼ cups of sugar.

❦ Boil these together in a preserving
pan for approximately 30 minutes,
removing any scum that may surface.
When the setting point is reached,
pour into warm jars and seal tightly.

A BASKET OF SHINING RED APPLES SYMBOLIZES THE
BEGINNING OF FALL

Where the apple reddens
Never pry –
Lest we lose our Edens,
Eve and I.

Robert Browning

Apple Butter

This is a wonderful way to use up windfall apples, although this recipe gives cooking apples as a basic. The butter improves with keeping for up to a year. It should turn out firm on the outside with a golden, melting, juicy center.

INGREDIENTS

4lb. Cooking Apples
1¾ cups Sweet Cider
7 cups Sugar
1 t. Ground Cinnamon

METHOD

❧ Wash the apples and cut in half; do not worry about removing the skin or seeds. Place the fruit in a preserving pan and pour over the cider. Cook until the fruit is very soft and pulpy, then remove from the heat and pass through a sieve.

❧ Return the apple to the clean preserving pan and continue to cook slowly, then add the sugar and ground cinnamon, stirring to make sure all the sugar dissolves.

❧ When the butter is thick and coats the back of a wooden spoon with a sugary solution, it is ready for potting.

Prune Conserve

Prunes were very popular with the Victorians. They enjoyed a reputation for medicinal effectiveness, were used in tarts and "molds," and were considered particularly good for children. This conserve is more suited to the adult palate; it is delectable but a little goes a long way.

INGREDIENTS

2¼ cups Pitted Prunes
5 cups Fresh Darjeeling Tea
2¼ cups Caster Sugar
1 Fresh Lemon

METHOD

❧ Place the prunes in a bowl and pour the freshly-made tea over them; allow to stand for several hours.

❧ When well soaked, transfer to a preserving pan and boil until the prunes become soft. Slowly stir in the sugar, making sure it has fully dissolved, then add the lemon juice and rind and boil until setting point is reached.

❧ Pot and seal tightly.

WINE JELLY

Good wine is a good familiar creature if it be well used.

WILLIAM SHAKESPEARE

HERB JELLY

Herb jellies are a good way to serve herbs from your garden all
year round. Taste the jelly for the strength of its flavor before adding
the chopped fresh herbs, so that you can modify the amount you
add; it should not be overpoweringly strong.

INGREDIENTS

4lb. Green Cooking Apples

A Good Handful of
Your Favorite Herb
(e.g., Mint, Rosemary, Thyme, Sage)

Fresh Water

Juice of 1 Lemon

Sugar

METHOD

❧ Wash the apples thoroughly and cut them up (you
do not have to remove the seeds or core). Place them
in a preserving pan with half of the herbs and cover with water. Bring
to the boil and simmer until the fruit is soft.

❧ Pour the contents of the pan into a jelly bag and strain off the juice
for several hours. Measure the juice and return to the pan to reheat,
and add $2^{1/4}$ cups of sugar for each $2^{1/2}$ cups of juice and stir to
dissolve completely.

❧ Finely chop the remaining herbs and add them to the pan.
Continue boiling until setting point is reached.

❧ Pour into warm jars and seal tightly.

ℐNDEX